PERCY JACKSON
MAD LIBS®

by L

An Imprint of Penguin

MAD LIBS
Penguin Young Readers Group
An Imprint of Penguin Random House LLC

Mad Libs format copyright © 2017 by Penguin Random House LLC. All rights reserved.

Concept created by Roger Price & Leonard Stern.

© Rick Riordan

Published by Mad Libs,
an imprint of Penguin Random House LLC,
345 Hudson Street, New York, New York 10014.
Printed in the USA.

ISBN 9780515159554
3 5 7 9 10 8 6 4

MAD LIBS

INSTRUCTIONS

MAD LIBS® is a game for people who don't like games! It can be played by one, two, three, four, or forty.

● RIDICULOUSLY SIMPLE DIRECTIONS

In this tablet you will find stories containing blank spaces where words are left out. One player, the READER, selects one of these stories. The READER does not tell anyone what the story is about. Instead, he/she asks the other players, the WRITERS, to give him/her words. These words are used to fill in the blank spaces in the story.

● TO PLAY

The READER asks each WRITER in turn to call out a word—an adjective or a noun or whatever the space calls for—and uses them to fill in the blank spaces in the story. The result is a MAD LIBS® game.

When the READER then reads the completed MAD LIBS® game to the other players, they will discover that they have written a story that is fantastic, screamingly funny, shocking, silly, crazy, or just plain dumb—depending upon which words each WRITER called out.

● EXAMPLE (*Before* and *After*)

"_____!" he said _____
    EXCLAMATION   ADVERB

as he jumped into his convertible _____ and
                                       NOUN

drove off with his _____ wife.
                      ADJECTIVE

"__OUCH__!" he said __STUPIDLY__
    EXCLAMATION   ADVERB

as he jumped into his convertible __CAT__ and
                                     NOUN

drove off with his __BRAVE__ wife.
                      ADJECTIVE

QUICK REVIEW

In case you have forgotten what adjectives, adverbs, nouns, and verbs are, here is a quick review:

An ADJECTIVE describes something or somebody. *Lumpy*, *soft*, *ugly*, *messy*, and *short* are adjectives.

An ADVERB tells how something is done. It modifies a verb and usually ends in "ly." *Modestly*, *stupidly*, *greedily*, and *carefully* are adverbs.

A NOUN is the name of a person, place, or thing. *Sidewalk*, *umbrella*, *bridle*, *bathtub*, and *nose* are nouns.

A VERB is an action word. *Run*, *pitch*, *jump*, and *swim* are verbs. Put the verbs in past tense if the directions say PAST TENSE. *Ran*, *pitched*, *jumped*, and *swam* are verbs in the past tense.

When we ask for A PLACE, we mean any sort of place: a country or city (*Spain*, *Cleveland*) or a room (*bathroom*, *kitchen*).

An EXCLAMATION or SILLY WORD is any sort of funny sound, gasp, grunt, or outcry, like *Wow!*, *Ouch!*, *Whomp!*, *Ick!*, and *Gadzooks!*

When we ask for specific words, like a NUMBER, a COLOR, an ANIMAL, or a PART OF THE BODY, we mean a word that is one of those things, like *seven*, *blue*, *horse*, or *head*.

When we ask for a PLURAL, it means more than one. For example, *cat* pluralized is *cats*.

MAD LIBS® is fun to play with friends, but you can also play it by yourself! To begin with, DO NOT look at the story on the page below. Fill in the blanks on this page with the words called for. Then, using the words you have selected, fill in the blank spaces in the story.

Now you've created your own hilarious MAD LIBS® game!

PERCY'S PATH

NOUN _____

NOUN _____

NOUN _____

NOUN _____

NOUN _____

CELEBRITY (MALE) _____

PLURAL NOUN _____

NOUN _____

PART OF THE BODY _____

PERSON IN ROOM (FEMALE) _____

NOUN _____

ADJECTIVE _____

ADJECTIVE _____

ADJECTIVE _____

MAD LIBS

PERCY'S PATH

Look, I didn't want to be a half-_____. I was just a twelve-
<u>NOUN</u>

year-old _____, minding his own business, trying to get by at
<u>NOUN</u>

boarding school, when my _____ got turned upside down.
<u>NOUN</u>

My _____ teacher tried to kill me, I found out my best friend
<u>NOUN</u>

was a/an _____, and most surprising of all, I discovered my
<u>NOUN</u>

real father was _____, god of the sea. Not only that, but I
<u>CELEBRITY (MALE)</u>

had to help save the _____ of Olympus from the evil
<u>PLURAL NOUN</u>

_____, Kronos. It was enough to make my _____
<u>NOUN</u>   <u>PART OF THE BODY</u>

spin. Along the way, to complicate matters, I got a crush on my friend,

_____, the daughter of Athena, goddess of
<u>PERSON IN ROOM (FEMALE)</u>

_____. Yeah, life as a/an _____-blood is pretty
<u>NOUN</u>   <u>ADJECTIVE</u>

dangerous, and most of the time, it gets you killed in _____
                                                 <u>ADJECTIVE</u>

ways. But, if you're lucky, you might just help save _____
                                                  <u>ADJECTIVE</u>

civilization as we know it.

From PERCY JACKSON MAD LIBS® • © Rick Riordan.
Published in 2017 by Mad Libs, an imprint of Penguin Random House LLC.

MAD LIBS® is fun to play with friends, but you can also play it by yourself! To begin with, DO NOT look at the story on the page below. Fill in the blanks on this page with the words called for. Then, using the words you have selected, fill in the blank spaces in the story.

Now you've created your own hilarious MAD LIBS® game!

THE LIGHTNING THIEF

NOUN _____

ADVERB _____

NOUN _____

LAST NAME _____

NOUN _____

NOUN _____

NOUN _____

ADJECTIVE _____

NOUN _____

NOUN _____

PLURAL NOUN _____

A PLACE _____

PLURAL NOUN _____

ADJECTIVE _____

The prophecy: *You shall go west, and face the* _____ *who has*
                                                    NOUN

turned. You shall find what was stolen, and see it _____ *returned.*
                                                        ADVERB

You shall be betrayed by one who calls you a/an _____. *And you*
                                                    NOUN

shall fail to save what matters most, in the end.

When Percy Jackson is kicked out of Yancy Academy after calling

Mr. _____ an "old _____," he finds himself at
       LAST NAME   NOUN

Camp Half-Blood. There, he discovers he is part god, part

_____, and that his father is Poseidon, god of the
   NOUN

_____. He is then sent on a/an _____ quest to find
   NOUN   ADJECTIVE

Zeus's stolen lightning _____ and return it before the summer
                            NOUN

solstice. There to help him along the way are Grover, a satyr, who has

the upper body of a boy and the lower body of a/an _____,
                                                        NOUN

and Annabeth, daughter of Athena, the goddess of wisdom, war, and

_____. Together, they travel across (the) _____,
   PLURAL NOUN   A PLACE

defeating monsters, fighting _____, and traveling to the
                                 PLURAL NOUN

depths of the underworld—all in the name of preventing a/an

_____ war.
   ADJECTIVE

From PERCY JACKSON MAD LIBS® • © Rick Riordan.
Published in 2017 by Mad Libs, an imprint of Penguin Random House LLC.

MAD LIBS® is fun to play with friends, but you can also play it by yourself! To begin with, DO NOT look at the story on the page below. Fill in the blanks on this page with the words called for. Then, using the words you have selected, fill in the blank spaces in the story.

Now you've created your own hilarious MAD LIBS® game!

GOOD OL' GROVER

PART OF THE BODY _____

PART OF THE BODY _____

NOUN _____

PLURAL NOUN _____

PART OF THE BODY (PLURAL) _____

A PLACE _____

A PLACE _____

CELEBRITY _____

NOUN _____

NOUN _____

ADVERB _____

PLURAL NOUN _____

PLURAL NOUN _____

PART OF THE BODY _____

PLURAL NOUN _____

NOUN _____

MAD LIBS®

GOOD OL' GROVER

Percy's best friend, Grover, is a satyr, which means he has the

_____ of a man and the _____ of a goat. He was
PART OF THE BODY   PART OF THE BODY

stationed at the Yancy Academy when he discovered Percy was a half-

_____. The two have been thick as _____ ever
NOUN   PLURAL NOUN

since. In fact, Grover and Percy have an empathy link, which means

they can communicate with their _____ even when
PART OF THE BODY (PLURAL)

Grover is in (the) _____ and Percy is in (the) _____.
A PLACE   A PLACE

This comes in handy when Grover is off on his lifelong quest to

track down the god _____, lord of the _____. Like
CELEBRITY   NOUN

all satyrs, Grover can play music on his _____ pipes, and
NOUN

when he plays _____, he can read messages written in
ADVERB

_____. Grover can also smell _____ from a
PLURAL NOUN   PLURAL NOUN

mile away. And he will also eat pretty much anything you put in front

of his _____, from tin cans to _____—but if you
PART OF THE BODY   PLURAL NOUN

want Grover on your good side, just serve him a piping hot plate

of _____ enchiladas. Yum!
NOUN

From PERCY JACKSON MAD LIBS® • © Rick Riordan.
Published in 2017 by Mad Libs, an imprint of Penguin Random House LLC.

MAD LIBS® is fun to play with friends, but you can also play it by yourself! To begin with, DO NOT look at the story on the page below. Fill in the blanks on this page with the words called for. Then, using the words you have selected, fill in the blank spaces in the story.

Now you've created your own hilarious MAD LIBS® game!

ATTAGIRL, ANNABETH

PLURAL NOUN _____

NOUN _____

NOUN _____

NOUN _____

NOUN _____

NOUN _____

PLURAL NOUN _____

PLURAL NOUN _____

A PLACE _____

PART OF THE BODY (PLURAL) _____

NOUN _____

NOUN _____

PLURAL NOUN _____

MAD LIBS®

ATTAGIRL, ANNABETH

Annabeth Chase is the daughter of Athena, the goddess of wisdom and

_____—and the apple doesn't fall far from the
PLURAL NOUN

_____. Annabeth is as smart as a/an _____. She ran
NOUN   NOUN

away from home when she was just a young _____ because
NOUN

she didn't get along with her father and step-_____. As a
NOUN

result, she has been at Camp Half-_____ longer than anyone
NOUN

else—which makes her the perfect person to show Percy the

_____ when he arrives. Annabeth wants to be an architect
PLURAL NOUN

when she grows up, so that she can build _____ all over
PLURAL NOUN

(the) _____. Annabeth is great to have around in battle,
A PLACE

because she is excellent at thinking on her _____.
PART OF THE BODY (PLURAL)

And, while Percy is a brave and strong _____, as Annabeth
NOUN

herself might say, he can sometimes be a seaweed _____. As a
NOUN

result, she and Percy make a good pair of _____.
PLURAL NOUN

MAD LIBS® is fun to play with friends, but you can also play it by yourself! To begin with, DO NOT look at the story on the page below. Fill in the blanks on this page with the words called for. Then, using the words you have selected, fill in the blank spaces in the story.

Now you've created your own hilarious MAD LIBS® game!

THE CAMPERS

PLURAL NOUN _____

PLURAL NOUN _____

PLURAL NOUN _____

NOUN _____

PLURAL NOUN _____

NOUN _____

PLURAL NOUN _____

CELEBRITY _____

PLURAL NOUN _____

PLURAL NOUN _____

NOUN _____

PERSON IN ROOM _____

PART OF THE BODY (PLURAL) _____

NOUN _____

ADVERB _____

PLURAL NOUN _____

MAD LIBS®

THE CAMPERS

You've met Grover and Annabeth, but who are the other

_____ at Camp Half-Blood?
   PLURAL NOUN

Luke Castellan is the son of Hermes, god of _____. He leaves
                                                PLURAL NOUN

camp to fight on the side of Kronos, king of the _____.
                                                  PLURAL NOUN

Clarisse La Rue, daughter of Ares, the _____ of war, is tough
                                              NOUN

as _____ and isn't afraid to fight a/an _____.
     PLURAL NOUN   NOUN

Silena Beauregard is the daughter of Aphrodite, goddess of love and

_____.
   PLURAL NOUN

Charles Beckendorf, son of _____, the god of
                                      CELEBRITY

_____, can build _____ out of metal and can
   PLURAL NOUN   PLURAL NOUN

fix any _____.
          NOUN

Connor and Travis Stoll are brothers and the sons of _____.
                                                          PERSON IN ROOM

They always have a mischievous gleam in their _____.
                                               PART OF THE BODY (PLURAL)

Thalia Grace, the daughter of Zeus, got turned into a/an

_____, but once she came back, she fought _____
   NOUN   ADVERB

alongside Percy and his _____.
                           PLURAL NOUN

From PERCY JACKSON MAD LIBS® • © Rick Riordan.
Published in 2017 by Mad Libs, an imprint of Penguin Random House LLC.

MAD LIBS® is fun to play with friends, but you can also play it by yourself! To begin with, DO NOT look at the story on the page below. Fill in the blanks on this page with the words called for. Then, using the words you have selected, fill in the blank spaces in the story.

Now you've created your own hilarious MAD LIBS® game!

THE SEA OF MONSTERS

NOUN _____

VERB _____

NOUN _____

VERB _____

ADJECTIVE _____

PLURAL NOUN _____

NOUN _____

PART OF THE BODY _____

NOUN _____

ADJECTIVE _____

NOUN _____

NOUN _____

ADJECTIVE _____

NOUN _____

PLURAL NOUN _____

The prophecy: *You shall sail the iron* _____ *with warriors of*
NOUN

bone. You shall find what you _____ *and make it your own. But*
VERB

despair for your _____ *entombed within stone, and fail without*
NOUN

friends, to _____ *home alone.*
VERB

Percy has a/an _____ friend at his new school named Tyson.
ADJECTIVE

When Percy is attacked by eight-foot-tall _____ during a
PLURAL NOUN

game of _____-ball, Tyson saves Percy's _____ and,
NOUN   PART OF THE BODY

along with Annabeth, the three return to Camp

Half-_____. There, the _____ tree that protects the
NOUN   ADJECTIVE

camp has been poisoned, and the new camp director, Tantalus, sends

bully Clarisse to find the Golden _____ to save the camp.
NOUN

Meanwhile, Percy discovers that Tyson is his half-brother, a Cyclops,

son of Poseidon and a/an _____. Percy, Annabeth, and Tyson
NOUN

run away from camp in order to find their friend Grover, whom they

believe has already found the _____ Fleece. They reunite with
ADJECTIVE

Clarisse and fight tooth and _____ to save the camp from the
NOUN

evil _____ that threaten it.
PLURAL NOUN

MAD LIBS® is fun to play with friends, but you can also play it by yourself! To begin with, DO NOT look at the story on the page below. Fill in the blanks on this page with the words called for. Then, using the words you have selected, fill in the blank spaces in the story.

Now you've created your own hilarious MAD LIBS® game!

THE BIG THREE

PLURAL NOUN _____

A PLACE _____

ADJECTIVE _____

NOUN _____

VERB _____

PLURAL NOUN _____

PLURAL NOUN _____

FIRST NAME (FEMALE) _____

NOUN _____

SAME NOUN _____

ADJECTIVE _____

NOUN _____

CELEBRITY _____

ADJECTIVE _____

NOUN _____

NOUN _____

ARTICLE OF CLOTHING _____

MAD LIBS

THE BIG THREE

The three most powerful _____ in (the) _____
PLURAL NOUN   A PLACE

were the _____ brothers Zeus, Poseidon, and Hades.
              ADJECTIVE

Zeus was the supreme _____ of the Olympians. He ruled the
                                 NOUN

sky and decided whether the sun would _____ or whether it
                                          VERB

was going to rain cats and _____. Zeus also ruled all of the
                                   PLURAL NOUN

_____ on earth. He was married to the goddess
PLURAL NOUN

_____.
FIRST NAME (FEMALE)

Poseidon ruled over the sea with a powerful weapon called a/an

_____. He used his _____ to cause earthquakes
     NOUN   SAME NOUN

when he felt _____. He lived in a/an _____ under
                 ADJECTIVE   NOUN

the sea with his wife, _____.
                               CELEBRITY

Hades is the _____ god of the underworld and the ruler of
                 ADJECTIVE

wealth and _____. He lives beneath the earth in a subterranean
                NOUN

_____. His magic _____ makes the wearer
    NOUN   ARTICLE OF CLOTHING

invisible.

From PERCY JACKSON MAD LIBS® • © Rick Riordan.
Published in 2017 by Mad Libs, an imprint of Penguin Random House LLC.

MAD LIBS® is fun to play with friends, but you can also play it by yourself! To begin with, DO NOT look at the story on the page below. Fill in the blanks on this page with the words called for. Then, using the words you have selected, fill in the blank spaces in the story.

Now you've created your own hilarious MAD LIBS® game!

A DAY AT CAMP HALF-BLOOD

NOUN _____

ADJECTIVE _____

ADJECTIVE _____

PLURAL NOUN _____

ADJECTIVE _____

NOUN _____

PLURAL NOUN _____

ANIMAL _____

CELEBRITY _____

NOUN _____

PLURAL NOUN _____

NOUN _____

SAME NOUN _____

PART OF THE BODY _____

MAD LIBS
A DAY AT CAMP HALF-BLOOD

You've got a whole day ahead of you at Camp Half-_____.
                                                        NOUN
But what activities will you partake in? Here are just some of your

_____ options:
   ADJECTIVE

Swordplay: Practice sparring with a/an _____ partner in the
                                                ADJECTIVE
arena.

Strawberry Picking: Pick fresh _____ while a satyr plays
                                        PLURAL NOUN
a/an _____ tune on a reed pipe.
        ADJECTIVE

Canoeing: Row, row, row your _____ in the lake for this
                                        NOUN
peaceful activity.

Archery: Get out your bow and _____ and see if you can
                                        PLURAL NOUN
aim them directly into the _____'s-eye.
                                ANIMAL

Arts and Crafts: Carve _____'s likeness in marble.
                                CELEBRITY

Climbing: This isn't your _____'s climbing wall! Dodge lava
                                    NOUN
and falling _____ as you make your way to the top.
                PLURAL NOUN

_____-back Riding: Gallop around on a/an _____
   NOUN   SAME NOUN
as the wind blows through your _____.
                                PART OF THE BODY

MAD LIBS® is fun to play with friends, but you can also play it by yourself! To begin with, DO NOT look at the story on the page below. Fill in the blanks on this page with the words called for. Then, using the words you have selected, fill in the blank spaces in the story.

Now you've created your own hilarious MAD LIBS® game!

CRAZY KRONOS

PLURAL NOUN _____

NOUN _____

VERB _____

PLURAL NOUN _____

A PLACE _____

ADJECTIVE _____

A PLACE _____

NOUN _____

PLURAL NOUN _____

ADJECTIVE _____

PLURAL NOUN _____

PLURAL NOUN _____

ADJECTIVE _____

VERB _____

PLURAL NOUN _____

NOUN _____

MAD LIBS

CRAZY KRONOS

Kronos, king of the _____, is a very powerful and evil
                          PLURAL NOUN

_____. He also controls time, meaning he can make it
NOUN

_____ faster or slower. Kronos has been looking for revenge
VERB

ever since his son, Zeus, cut him into a thousand _____,
                                                      PLURAL NOUN

tossing his remains into the darkest pit of (the) _____. The
                                                   A PLACE

Titan army was scattered, their _____ fortress destroyed, and
                                 ADJECTIVE

their allies were driven to the farthest corners of (the) _____.
                                                          A PLACE

Now, Kronos's _____ is healing, and he hungers for
               NOUN

_____. He wants to start a/an _____ war with the
PLURAL NOUN   ADJECTIVE

Olympian _____. As Kronos regains strength, he finds his
          PLURAL NOUN

way into the nightmares of _____, awakening _____
                            PLURAL NOUN   ADJECTIVE

monsters. Like the Olympian gods, Kronos is immortal, meaning he

can never _____—unless Percy and his _____
           VERB   PLURAL NOUN

can destroy his _____.
                 NOUN

From PERCY JACKSON MAD LIBS® • © Rick Riordan.
Published in 2017 by Mad Libs, an imprint of Penguin Random House LLC.

MAD LIBS® is fun to play with friends, but you can also play it by yourself! To begin with, DO NOT look at the story on the page below. Fill in the blanks on this page with the words called for. Then, using the words you have selected, fill in the blank spaces in the story.

Now you've created your own hilarious MAD LIBS® game!

THE TITAN'S CURSE

NOUN _____

A PLACE _____

NOUN _____

PLURAL NOUN _____

NOUN _____

NOUN _____

VERB ENDING IN "ING" _____

PERSON IN ROOM (FEMALE) _____

PERSON IN ROOM (MALE) _____

NOUN _____

NOUN _____

A PLACE _____

ADJECTIVE _____

VERB ENDING IN "ING" _____

ADJECTIVE _____

MAD LIBS

THE TITAN'S CURSE

The prophecy: *Five shall go west to the* _____ *in chains. One*
NOUN

shall be lost in (the) _____ *without rain. The* _____ *of*
A PLACE   NOUN

Olympus shows the trail. Campers and _____ *combined*
PLURAL NOUN

prevail. The _____ *'s curse must one withstand, and one shall*
NOUN

perish by a/an _____ *'s hand.*
NOUN

Percy, Thalia, and Annabeth travel to a/an _____
VERB ENDING IN "ING"

school in Maine to help Grover rescue two powerful demigod siblings,

_____ and _____, when they are
PERSON IN ROOM (FEMALE)   PERSON IN ROOM (MALE)

attacked by a manticore named Dr. _____. Luckily, Artemis,
NOUN

goddess of the _____, and her hunters rescue the demigods—
NOUN

but not before the Great Stirring of Monsters is unleashed upon (the)

_____ by the _____ god, Kronos. Artemis goes off to
A PLACE   ADJECTIVE

stop the Great _____, and Percy must sneak away
VERB ENDING IN "ING"

from camp to help his friends assist Artemis in her _____
ADJECTIVE

quest.

From PERCY JACKSON MAD LIBS® • © Rick Riordan.
Published in 2017 by Mad Libs, an imprint of Penguin Random House LLC.

MAD LIBS® is fun to play with friends, but you can also play it by yourself! To begin with, DO NOT look at the story on the page below. Fill in the blanks on this page with the words called for. Then, using the words you have selected, fill in the blank spaces in the story.

Now you've created your own hilarious MAD LIBS® game!

YOUR PROPHECY FROM THE ORACLE

ADJECTIVE _____

NOUN _____

NOUN _____

PART OF THE BODY (PLURAL) _____

ADVERB _____

ADJECTIVE _____

VERB _____

NOUN _____

PART OF THE BODY _____

VERB _____

NOUN _____

VERB ENDING IN "ING" _____

NOUN _____

NOUN _____

PART OF THE BODY _____

NOUN _____

PART OF THE BODY _____

NOUN _____

Now it's *your* turn to go on a/an _____ quest. You climb the

ADJECTIVE

stairs of the Big _____ to the attic, which is filled with more

NOUN

Greek hero junk than you can throw a/an _____ at. There, by

NOUN

the window, is the most gruesome sight your _____

PART OF THE BODY (PLURAL)

have ever seen: the Oracle. Mist swirls _____ around her, and

ADVERB

suddenly, you hear these _____ words: *You shall* _____

ADJECTIVE VERB

in a/an _____ *in a place like no other. You shall discover your*

NOUN

_____ *and* _____ *with another. You shall question a/*

PART OF THE BODY VERB

an _____ *that you know to be true. And you shall succeed at*

NOUN

_____ *with a/an* _____, *too.* Then, quick as

VERB ENDING IN "ING" NOUN

a/an _____, the Oracle's _____ closes tight, as if it

NOUN PART OF THE BODY

hadn't been open in a hundred years. The attic is quiet as a/an

_____, and your _____ is riddled with questions.

NOUN PART OF THE BODY

Hopefully Chiron can shine a/an _____ on this mystery . . .

NOUN

Published in 2017 by Mad Libs, an imprint of Penguin Random House LLC.

MAD LIBS® is fun to play with friends, but you can also play it by yourself! To begin with, DO NOT look at the story on the page below. Fill in the blanks on this page with the words called for. Then, using the words you have selected, fill in the blank spaces in the story.

Now you've created your own hilarious MAD LIBS® game!

OH, GODS, PART 1

PLURAL NOUN _____

NOUN _____

ADJECTIVE _____

PLURAL NOUN _____

VERB _____

PLURAL NOUN _____

PLURAL NOUN _____

NOUN _____

NOUN _____

PLURAL NOUN _____

MAD LIBS®

OH, GODS, PART 1

Zeus, Poseidon, and Hades may have been the Big Three

_____, but the rest of the Greek gods are still a/an

PLURAL NOUN

_____ to be reckoned with.

NOUN

Ares, the god of war, had a/an _____ personality and was

ADJECTIVE

unpopular with the other gods and _____.

PLURAL NOUN

Athena taught humans how to weave, sew, and _____. She

VERB

was the goddess of wisdom, skill, and war.

Hestia was the goddess of hearth and home. She provided warmth and

security for _____ by keeping fires in their _____.

PLURAL NOUN PLURAL NOUN

Aphrodite, the goddess of love and beauty, was known for her attractive

_____.

NOUN

Apollo was famous for playing music on his _____ and was

NOUN

the god of the sun, music, and _____.

PLURAL NOUN

From PERCY JACKSON MAD LIBS® • © Rick Riordan.
Published in 2017 by Mad Libs, an imprint of Penguin Random House LLC.

MAD LIBS® is fun to play with friends, but you can also play it by yourself! To begin with, DO NOT look at the story on the page below. Fill in the blanks on this page with the words called for. Then, using the words you have selected, fill in the blank spaces in the story.

Now you've created your own hilarious MAD LIBS® game!

OH, GODS, PART 2

PLURAL NOUN _____

PLURAL NOUN _____

PLURAL NOUN _____

A PLACE _____

TYPE OF LIQUID _____

NOUN _____

PART OF THE BODY _____

PLURAL NOUN _____

ADJECTIVE _____

PLURAL NOUN _____

PLURAL NOUN _____

PART OF THE BODY (PLURAL) _____

PLURAL NOUN _____

Artemis, the goddess of the hunt and the moon, loved to hunt

_____ with a bow and _____.
　　PLURAL NOUN　　　　　　　　　　　　　PLURAL NOUN

Demeter taught humans how to grow _____. She was the
　　　　　　　　　　　　　　　　　　　　PLURAL NOUN

goddess of agriculture and was the source of all life in (the)

_____.
　A PLACE

Dionysus, the god of _____, was lighthearted and always
　　　　　　　　　　　　TYPE OF LIQUID

helpful to a/an _____ in need.
　　　　　　　　NOUN

Hephaestus did not have a very attractive _____, but he was
　　　　　　　　　　　　　　　　　　　　　PART OF THE BODY

kind and lovable. He was the god of fire and _____.
　　　　　　　　　　　　　　　　　　　　　PLURAL NOUN

Hera, the _____ wife of Zeus, was the goddess of marriage
　　　　　ADJECTIVE

and family and was known for being jealous of Zeus's _____.
　　　　　　　　　　　　　　　　　　　　　　　　　PLURAL NOUN

Hermes, messenger for the _____, had wings on his
　　　　　　　　　　　　　　　PLURAL NOUN

_____. He was the god of travelers, merchants,
PART OF THE BODY (PLURAL)

and _____.
　　PLURAL NOUN

MAD LIBS® is fun to play with friends, but you can also play it by yourself! To begin with, DO NOT look at the story on the page below. Fill in the blanks on this page with the words called for. Then, using the words you have selected, fill in the blank spaces in the story.

Now you've created your own hilarious MAD LIBS® game!

THE BATTLE OF THE LABYRINTH

VERB _____

NOUN _____

NOUN _____

CELEBRITY _____

NOUN _____

NOUN _____

ADJECTIVE _____

PERSON IN ROOM (FEMALE) _____

PERSON IN ROOM (FEMALE) _____

PLURAL NOUN _____

ADJECTIVE _____

ADJECTIVE _____

ADJECTIVE _____

VERB ENDING IN "S" _____

VERB _____

CELEBRITY _____

PERSON IN ROOM (MALE) _____

PLURAL NOUN _____

MAD LIBS
THE BATTLE OF THE LABYRINTH

The prophecy: *You shall* _____ *in the darkness of the endless*
VERB

maze, the _____, *the traitor, and the lost one raise. You shall rise*
NOUN

or fall by the ghost _____'s *hand, the child of* _____'s
NOUN   CELEBRITY

final stand. Destroy with a/an _____'s *final breath, and lose*
NOUN

a/an _____ *to worse than death.*
NOUN

When Percy has his first day at yet another new school, he is attacked

by two _____ cheerleaders, _____ and
ADJECTIVE   PERSON IN ROOM (FEMALE)

_____, who turn out to be *empousai*, which is a fancy
PERSON IN ROOM (FEMALE)

word for monsters who feed on the blood of _____. Percy
PLURAL NOUN

escapes, finds Annabeth, and goes back to Camp _____-Blood.
ADJECTIVE

This time, Annabeth receives a/an _____ prophecy. With
ADJECTIVE

Percy, Grover, and Percy's half-brother, Tyson, by her side, she goes on

a/an _____ quest into the Labyrinth. (The Labyrinth is a
ADJECTIVE

maze that _____ and is very difficult to _____
VERB ENDING IN "S"   VERB

in.) Together, they must find _____, inventor of the
CELEBRITY

Labyrinth, to help them stop _____ and his army of
PERSON IN ROOM (MALE)

_____ before it's too late.
PLURAL NOUN

From PERCY JACKSON MAD LIBS® • © Rick Riordan.
Published in 2017 by Mad Libs, an imprint of Penguin Random House LLC.

MAD LIBS® is fun to play with friends, but you can also play it by yourself! To begin with, DO NOT look at the story on the page below. Fill in the blanks on this page with the words called for. Then, using the words you have selected, fill in the blank spaces in the story.

Now you've created your own hilarious MAD LIBS® game!

DEMIGOD DREAM

NOUN _____

NOUN _____

ADJECTIVE _____

NOUN _____

ANIMAL _____

SILLY WORD _____

SAME SILLY WORD _____

PART OF THE BODY _____

VERB ENDING IN "ING" _____

NOUN _____

PERSON IN ROOM _____

ARTICLE OF CLOTHING _____

PART OF THE BODY _____

YOUR NAME _____

ADVERB _____

VERB _____

NOUN _____

VERB _____

PART OF THE BODY _____

MAD LIBS

DEMIGOD DREAM

As any half-blood worth his or her _____ knows, dreams can
                                        NOUN

reveal important information about your _____. Here is *your*
                                              NOUN

_____ dream:
   ADJECTIVE

It's a dark and stormy _____, and you're driving down a
                              NOUN

bumpy road. You hear the cry of a/an _____: "_____!
                                          ANIMAL   SILLY WORD

_____!" it calls. Chills run up and down your _____.
SAME SILLY WORD   PART OF THE BODY

Suddenly, you come to a/an _____ halt, and you find
                              VERB ENDING IN "ING"

yourself standing in front of a/an _____ shrouded in mist.
                                        NOUN

You walk inside and see your dear friend _____ wearing a/an
                                              PERSON IN ROOM

_____ on his/her _____. "Help me,
ARTICLE OF CLOTHING   PART OF THE BODY

_____!" your friend says _____. "I can't
  YOUR NAME   ADVERB

_____!" Before you can reply, you're yanked out of sleep.
   VERB

"Good morning, sleepy _____!" says your mother. "It's time
                            NOUN

to rise and _____!" You scratch your _____ in
               VERB   PART OF THE BODY

confusion. Whatever did your dream mean?

MAD LIBS® is fun to play with friends, but you can also play it by yourself! To begin with, DO NOT look at the story on the page below. Fill in the blanks on this page with the words called for. Then, using the words you have selected, fill in the blank spaces in the story.

Now you've created your own hilarious MAD LIBS® game!

QUIZ:
ARE YOU A HALF-BLOOD?

ADJECTIVE _____

NOUN _____

PART OF THE BODY _____

PLURAL NOUN _____

VERB _____

PERSON IN ROOM _____

PERSON IN ROOM _____

PART OF THE BODY _____

PLURAL NOUN _____

MAD LIBS®
QUIZ:
ARE YOU A HALF-BLOOD?

To discover whether you are a/an _____ demigod, read the
ADJECTIVE

statements below and circle YES or NO:

- When you try to pay attention to your _____ teacher,
  NOUN
  you often find your _____ wandering.
  PART OF THE BODY
  Answer: YES/NO

- You have difficulty reading books about _____.
  PLURAL NOUN
  Answer: YES/NO

- You often wonder how it is possible that you are related to your
  parents because they _____ very differently from you.
  VERB
  Answer: YES/NO

- At least one of your good friends, like _____ or
  PERSON IN ROOM
  _____, doesn't seem quite normal—like maybe
  PERSON IN ROOM
  they have horns growing out of their _____.
  PART OF THE BODY
  Answer: YES/NO

- You have an irrational fear of _____.
  PLURAL NOUN
  Answer: YES/NO

If you answered YES to all of these questions, you may be a half-blood!

From PERCY JACKSON MAD LIBS® • © Rick Riordan.
Published in 2017 by Mad Libs, an imprint of Penguin Random House LLC.

MAD LIBS® is fun to play with friends, but you can also play it by yourself! To begin with, DO NOT look at the story on the page below. Fill in the blanks on this page with the words called for. Then, using the words you have selected, fill in the blank spaces in the story.

Now you've created your own hilarious MAD LIBS® game!

HOW TO USE THE MIST, BY CHIRON

ADJECTIVE _____

ADJECTIVE _____

PLURAL NOUN _____

ADJECTIVE _____

ADJECTIVE _____

PERSON IN ROOM _____

NOUN _____

PLURAL NOUN _____

NOUN _____

PLURAL NOUN _____

PERSON IN ROOM _____

PERSON IN ROOM _____

PART OF THE BODY (PLURAL) _____

PART OF THE BODY _____

ADJECTIVE _____

VERB ENDING IN "ING" _____

VERB _____

MAD LIBS®
HOW TO USE THE MIST,
BY CHIRON

Greetings, _____ student. I am Chiron, centaur and son of
           ADJECTIVE

the _____ Titan, Kronos. I train half- _____ such
    ADJECTIVE   PLURAL NOUN

as yourself, but I only teach a few very _____ students how to
                                          ADJECTIVE

use the Mist, which gods and demigods conjure to hide our world from

_____ mortals. I think that you, _____, have what it
ADJECTIVE   PERSON IN ROOM

takes. Now, first, you must focus on what the mortal *wants* to see. So,

for example, if a/an _____ has just attacked your school
                           NOUN

cafeteria, you must project a normal lunchroom scene. Picture

_____ serving macaroni and _____ and pizza
PLURAL NOUN   NOUN

with _____ on top. Imagine the school bully,
         PLURAL NOUN

_____, giving _____ a wedgie. Then, sharply snap
PERSON IN ROOM   PERSON IN ROOM

your _____. A gust of Mist will escape from your
     PART OF THE BODY (PLURAL)

_____ and surround the mortals, making them forget what
PART OF THE BODY

they have just witnessed. It may sound simple, but only the most

_____ demigods are capable of _____ with
ADJECTIVE   VERB ENDING IN "ING"

the Mist. Do you have the power to _____ within you?
                              VERB

MAD LIBS® is fun to play with friends, but you can also play it by yourself! To begin with, DO NOT look at the story on the page below. Fill in the blanks on this page with the words called for. Then, using the words you have selected, fill in the blank spaces in the story.

Now you've created your own hilarious MAD LIBS® game!

THE LAST OLYMPIAN

NOUN _____

NOUN _____

PART OF THE BODY _____

NOUN _____

NOUN _____

A PLACE _____

PERSON IN ROOM _____

PERSON IN ROOM (FEMALE) _____

PLURAL NOUN _____

ADVERB _____

ADJECTIVE _____

ADJECTIVE _____

PART OF THE BODY (PLURAL) _____

PART OF THE BODY (PLURAL) _____

PART OF THE BODY (PLURAL) _____

ADJECTIVE _____

VERB _____

A PLACE _____

MAD LIBS®

THE LAST OLYMPIAN

The prophecy: *A half-_____ of the eldest gods shall reach*
                          NOUN

sixteen against all odds and see the _____ in endless sleep. The
                                              NOUN

hero's _____, cursed _____ shall reap. A single
         PART OF THE BODY   NOUN

_____ shall end his days, (the) _____ to preserve or raze.
   NOUN   A PLACE

Percy and Charles Beckendorf fly off on _____, the pegasus,
                                          PERSON IN ROOM

to attack Luke's ship, the *Princess* _____, where
                                       PERSON IN ROOM (FEMALE)

Kronos's army of _____ were prepared to fight
                      PLURAL NOUN

_____. There is a/an _____ spy at Camp Half-
   ADVERB   ADJECTIVE

Blood. Meanwhile, the Olympian gods are fighting to contain

Typhon, an enormous monster with _____ skin, human
                                      ADJECTIVE

_____, the _____ of an eagle,
PART OF THE BODY (PLURAL)   PART OF THE BODY (PLURAL)

and scaly, reptilian _____. But Kronos's army grows
                      PART OF THE BODY (PLURAL)

more _____ every day, and Percy must convince the
        ADJECTIVE

Olympians to come together to _____ against him and save
                                    VERB

(the) _____ from his wrath.
         A PLACE

MAD LIBS® is fun to play with friends, but you can also play it by yourself! To begin with, DO NOT look at the story on the page below. Fill in the blanks on this page with the words called for. Then, using the words you have selected, fill in the blank spaces in the story.

Now you've created your own hilarious MAD LIBS® game!

OH, OH, OH, IT'S MAGIC

NOUN _____

NOUN _____

NOUN _____

PLURAL NOUN _____

NOUN _____

SILLY WORD _____

NOUN _____

PART OF THE BODY _____

NOUN _____

PART OF THE BODY (PLURAL) _____

VERB ENDING IN "ING" _____

PART OF THE BODY _____

MAD LIBS®

OH, OH, OH, IT'S MAGIC

Each demigod at Camp Half-Blood has their own special magic item

to aid them in camp games like Capture the _____, but also
                                              NOUN

for godly endeavors, like fighting a carnivorous _____ or a/an
                                                     NOUN

_____-eating horse. Here are just a few of the campers' trusty
    NOUN

_____:
  PLURAL NOUN

• Percy's magic item is Riptide, a sword made of Celestial

  _____, otherwise known as _____. When not
       NOUN   SILLY WORD

  in use, it is disguised as a ballpoint _____ that Percy keeps
                                              NOUN

  in his pocket.

• Annabeth has a magic Yankees baseball cap that, when she puts it

  on her _____, renders her invisible.
         PART OF THE BODY

• Thalia has a magical _____ called Aegis. As soon as
                            NOUN

  monsters or demigods lay their _____ on it,
                                   PART OF THE BODY (PLURAL)

  they run _____ in terror. When she's not using
           VERB ENDING IN "ING"

  Aegis, it appears on her _____ as a simple charm bracelet.
                            PART OF THE BODY

From PERCY JACKSON MAD LIBS® • © Rick Riordan.
Published in 2017 by Mad Libs, an imprint of Penguin Random House LLC.

MAD LIBS® is fun to play with friends, but you can also play it by yourself! To begin with, DO NOT look at the story on the page below. Fill in the blanks on this page with the words called for. Then, using the words you have selected, fill in the blank spaces in the story.

Now you've created your own hilarious MAD LIBS® game!

MEET THE MONSTERS, PART 1

ADJECTIVE _____

NOUN _____

NOUN _____

PART OF THE BODY (PLURAL) _____

NOUN _____

NOUN _____

PLURAL NOUN _____

ADJECTIVE _____

PART OF THE BODY (PLURAL) _____

PLURAL NOUN _____

PART OF THE BODY (PLURAL) _____

NOUN _____

PART OF THE BODY _____

ADJECTIVE _____

PLURAL NOUN _____

NOUN _____

ADJECTIVE _____

PART OF THE BODY (PLURAL) _____

Percy and his friends come across many a/an _____ monster
                                                  ADJECTIVE

on their adventures. Here are a few of the highlights:

• The **chimera** has the head of a/an _____, a/an
                                             NOUN

_____-caked mane, and the body and _____
   NOUN   PART OF THE BODY (PLURAL)

of a giant _____. It has a/an _____ growing out
              NOUN   NOUN

of its behind and breathes _____.
                               PLURAL NOUN

• The **hydra** is covered in _____ scales and has nine
                                 ADJECTIVE

_____, each covered in jagged _____.
PART OF THE BODY (PLURAL)   PLURAL NOUN

If it loses one of its _____, it just grows
                          PART OF THE BODY (PLURAL)

another one.

• The **manticore** has the body of a/an _____, a human
                                            NOUN

_____, and a/an _____ tail that shoots deadly
PART OF THE BODY   ADJECTIVE

_____.
PLURAL NOUN

• **Stymphalian birds** are _____-eating demon birds with
                               NOUN

_____ eyes and razor-sharp _____.
   ADJECTIVE   PART OF THE BODY (PLURAL)

MAD LIBS® is fun to play with friends, but you can also play it by yourself! To begin with, DO NOT look at the story on the page below. Fill in the blanks on this page with the words called for. Then, using the words you have selected, fill in the blank spaces in the story.

Now you've created your own hilarious MAD LIBS® game!

MEET THE MONSTERS, PART 2

ADJECTIVE _____

PLURAL NOUN _____

PERSON IN ROOM _____

ADJECTIVE _____

PLURAL NOUN _____

PART OF THE BODY _____

NOUN _____

A PLACE _____

NOUN _____

PART OF THE BODY (PLURAL) _____

PLURAL NOUN _____

PART OF THE BODY _____

PLURAL NOUN _____

TYPE OF LIQUID _____

More _____ monsters!

ADJECTIVE

- **Agrius and Oreius** are bear-men, the twin _____ of a

PLURAL NOUN

  bear and _____. They are eight feet tall, with

PERSON IN ROOM

  _____ chests, _____ for nails, and paws where

ADJECTIVE   PLURAL NOUN

  their _____ should be.

PART OF THE BODY

- **Cerberus** is a three-headed _____ the size of a woolly

NOUN

  mammoth. He guards the entrance to (the) _____.

A PLACE

- The **Clazmonian Sow** is an enormous winged _____

NOUN

  with bright pink _____. She destroys all the

PART OF THE BODY (PLURAL)

  _____ in her path and belches poison fire out of her

PLURAL NOUN

  _____.

PART OF THE BODY

- **Pit scorpions** are small compared to other monsters, but they can

  jump fifteen _____ into the air. They use their stingers

PLURAL NOUN

  to inject their victims with _____.

TYPE OF LIQUID